Code Queens: Narratives of Pioneering Women in Tech

"An Inspirational Tale of Women Changing the Face of Tech"

EVA C. MARTIN

CODE QUEENS

Copyright © 2024 by EVA C. MARTIN

All rights reserved. No part of this publication may be reproduced, distributed, or transmitted in any form or by any means, including photocopying, recording, or other electronic or mechanical methods, without the prior written permission of the publisher, except in the case of brief quotations embodied in critical reviews and certain other noncommercial uses permitted by copyright law.

TABLE OF CONTENT

FOREWORD 5
INTRODUCTION 6
    Shattering Boundaries in the Tech Sector: 6
Chapter 1: The First Code Queen, Ada Lovelace 8
    Life in the Early Years and Education: 8
    Working along with Charles Babbage: 9
    Contributions in the Field of Computing: 10
Chapter 2: The Pioneer of Programming, Grace Hopper .. 12
    Early Computer Work and a Career in the Navy: 12
    The creation of COBOL: 13
    An educational legacy in computer science: 14
Chapter 3: Margaret Hamilton, Head of the Apollo Guidance Computer 16
    The Apollo Missions Project: 16
    The Significance of Software Dependability: 17
    Later Developments in the Field of Software Engineering: 18
Chapter 4: Architect of the Internet, Radia Perlman 20
    The Spanning Tree Protocol's creation: 20
    Contributions to the Design of Networks: 21

    Thoughts on Women in Tech: 22

Chapter 5: Anita Borg, A Champion for Women in Computing 24

    Establishing the Center for Women and Technology: 24

    Establishment of the Grace Hopper Celebration: 25

    Ongoing Effect on Diversity in Technology: 26

Chapter 6: The Actress Who Became an Inventor, Hedy Lamarr 28

    The creation of the frequency-hopping spread spectrum: 28

    Appreciating the Contributions of Lamarr: 29

    The impact on Contemporary Wireless Communications: 30

Chapter 7: NASA's Trailblazing Katherine Johnson 32

    Determining Space Mission Trajectories: 32

    Apollo and Mercury Program Contributions: 33

    Recognition in the Following Years: 34

Chapter 8: The Gaming Pioneer, Carol Shaw 36

    Early Years of Video Game Development: 36

    Generation of Innovative Titles: 37

    Girl in Gaming: Obstacles and Triumphs: 38

Chapter 9: Search and Technology Innovator, Marissa Mayer 40

    Early Google Career: 40

    Yahoo!'s leadership!: 41

    Views Regarding Women in Leadership: 42

Chapter 10: Cryptography's Pioneer, Shafi Goldwasser ... 44

    A Contribution to the Theory of Complexity: 44

    Employment in Security and Cryptography: 45

    Acknowledgment and Trophy: 46

Chapter 11: Artificial Intelligence Leadership by Fei-Fei Li 48

    Studies on AI and Computer Vision: 48

    Google and Stanford Leadership: 49

    Promoting Ethical AI: 50

Chapter 12: Reshma Saujani, Encouraging Women in Tech 52

    Founders of Girls Who Code: 52

    Promoting Equity in STEM Education: 53

    Effect on Narrowing the Gender Gap in Tech: 54

Conclusion: Continuing the Tradition 56

Acknowledgments 58

About the Author 59

FOREWORD

This fascinating anthology, "Code Queens: Narratives of Pioneering Women in Tech," delves into the extraordinary lives of trailblazing females who have made a lasting impact on the technology industry.

Their tales serve as beacons of hope, shedding light on the route ahead for upcoming generations of would-be entrepreneurs as society develops.

From the revolutionary discoveries of Shafi Goldwasser in encryption to the visionary insights of Ada Lovelace, each story honors tenacity, inventiveness, and the unwavering will to challenge expectations.

As they pioneer a more diverse and dynamic tech scene, get ready to be moved by the bravery and intelligence of these Code Queens.

INTRODUCTION

Shattering Boundaries in the Tech Sector:

The experiences and voices of women have frequently been marginalized or ignored in the enormous history of technology.

However, these stories also include a tapestry of bravery, ingenuity, and resiliency that should be highlighted. "Narratives of Pioneering Women in Tech" aims to address this neglect by providing a forum for the trailblazers who, in spite of overwhelming obstacles, have changed and transformed the digital sector.

But there have been difficulties along the way. Systemic obstacles, varying from overt discrimination to subtle biases, have impeded the advancement and recognition of women in the technology industry. Their tenacity and resolve have not wavered in the face of these challenges.

Still, it's a long and difficult road to true diversity and equality in the tech industry. It necessitates building a climate of mutual respect, cooperation, and support in addition to tearing down ingrained prejudices and institutional hurdles.

With "Narratives of Pioneering Women in Tech," we hope to honor the accomplishments of women who have broken down barriers and made significant contributions to the IT industry.

Future generations can draw inspiration and encouragement from these stories, which serve as a timely reminder that diversity and inclusivity are not only moral requirements but also necessary components of creativity and advancement in the digital age.

CHAPTER 1: THE FIRST CODE QUEEN, ADA LOVELACE

Life in the Early Years and Education:

Ada Lovelace was the daughter of renowned poet Lord Byron and Lady Anne Isabella Milbanke. She was born Augusta Ada Byron on December 10, 1815, in London, England.

Ada was raised in an intellectually curious home under the strict supervision of her mother, who balanced Lord Byron's artistic impact with a demanding curriculum focused on science and arithmetic. Ada had health issues, yet even as a young child, she had a remarkable talent for arithmetic.

Her intense interest in Charles Babbage's Analytical Engine led to a fruitful partnership that resulted in the publication of her groundbreaking notes on the device in 1843.
Being acknowledged as the first computer programmer in history, Ada's forward-thinking ideas and creative thinking

created the foundation for contemporary computer programming, making her a trailblazing figure in the history of technology.

Working along with Charles Babbage:

The partnership between Ada Lovelace and Charles Babbage was revolutionary in the history of computers.

Lovelace was drawn to Babbage's innovative concepts and became fully committed to the Analytical Engine project. Their collaboration went beyond simple mentoring; Lovelace's sharp mind and aptitude for mathematics complimented Babbage's creative creativity.

Lovelace recognized the promise of Babbage's theoretical foundation for the Analytical Engine and imagined uses for it that went beyond simple computation.

Lovelace wrote some notes on the Analytical Engine in 1843, and in those notes he included what is regarded as the first algorithm designed to be run on a machine.

Her groundbreaking work established the groundwork for contemporary computer programming and demonstrated the revolutionary potential of creativity and teamwork in the still-developing field of computers.

Contributions in the Field of Computing:

Ada Lovelace made significant and groundbreaking contributions to the realm of computers.

Lovelace, the first computer programmer in history, left a lasting legacy of groundbreaking ideas that helped shape contemporary computing.

She was the first to realize that programming could go beyond basic numerical computations when she published her influential notes on Charles Babbage's Analytical Engine in 1843. Her notes detailed an algorithm created specifically for the machine.

Lovelace predicted that the Analytical Engine will be used to create pictures, music, and other media in addition to math problems. Long before electrical computers were invented, her vision and ingenuity showed how computational technology could be revolutionary.

Generations of technologists are still motivated by Lovelace's legacy, which highlights the significance of imagination and foresight in influencing the direction of computers.

CHAPTER 2: THE PIONEER OF PROGRAMMING, GRACE HOPPER

Early Computer Work and a Career in the Navy:

Grace Hopper's early computing work and naval career are prime examples of her extraordinary intelligence and pioneering zeal.

When Hopper was commissioned as a lieutenant in the US Navy during World War II, her technical prowess was immediately apparent.

She was given the task of working on the Harvard Mark I computer, where she made a substantial programming and debugging contribution.

Hopper stayed in the navy after the war and was instrumental in the creation of the UNIVAC I, one of the first commercial computers.

Her creation of the programming language compiler, which converted instructions similar to those in English into machine code, revolutionized programming and established the framework for contemporary software development.

Hopper's early computing accomplishments and naval career solidified her reputation as a technological leader and pioneer in computer science.

The creation of COBOL:

Grace Hopper's contribution to the development of COBOL (Common Business-Oriented Language) revolutionized the field of computer science.

In the late 1950s, Hopper led the effort to create COBOL, realizing the need for a universal programming language that could be understood across various computers and industries.

Drawing on her extensive programming experience and her keen understanding of user needs, Hopper played a central role in the design and implementation of COBOL, ensuring that it was user-friendly, efficient, and adaptable, making it the first widely used high-level programming language for business applications.

An educational legacy in computer science:

Grace Hopper left a huge legacy in computer science over her decades-long leadership and creativity.

Hopper was a trailblazer in the sector, and her innovations transformed computer education, software development, and programming languages.

Her contributions to the creation of the COBOL language changed the business computing environment by increasing its efficiency and accessibility.

Furthermore, Hopper's support of machine-independent programming resulted in the development of high-level programming languages, which helped to provide the foundation for contemporary software engineering techniques.

In addition to her technical accomplishments, Hopper broke down barriers for women in STEM fields and encouraged upcoming generations to work in the field.

Her lasting influence is still shaping computer science today, highlighting the value of creativity, diversity, and tenacity in fostering advancement and transformation.

CHAPTER 3: MARGARET HAMILTON, HEAD OF THE APOLLO GUIDANCE COMPUTER

The Apollo Missions Project:

Margaret Hamilton's reputation as a forerunner in computer science and software engineering was solidified by her crucial role in the Apollo missions.

In her capacity as the head of the MIT Instrumentation Laboratory's Software Engineering Division, Hamilton oversaw the group in charge of creating the onboard flight software for NASA's Apollo spacecraft.

Her creative approach to software design and strict testing procedures were crucial to the Apollo missions' success, which included the historic 1969 moon landing.

Hamilton became a trailblazer in the field of software engineering with her innovative work, which provided the groundwork for contemporary software engineering techniques. Her contributions to the Apollo program highlight the crucial nexus between technology and exploration and highlight how crucial rigorous software development is to accomplishing significant scientific milestones.

The Significance of Software Dependability:

Margaret Hamilton played a pivotal role in influencing the development of computer science and engineering through her emphasis on software reliability.

Her ground-breaking work on the Apollo missions as Director of the Software Engineering Division at MIT's Instrumentation Laboratory required software that was not only very inventive but also very dependable.

Hamilton's team implemented error-checking mechanisms and rigorous testing procedures to make sure the onboard flight software could handle the harsh circumstances of space travel.

The Apollo missions' triumph, which included the momentous moon landing, highlighted how crucial software dependability is for mission-critical systems.

Hamilton's groundbreaking work established the foundation for contemporary software engineering techniques and brought attention to the importance of fault tolerance, robustness, and dependability in the creation of intricate software systems.

Her impact lives on, influencing modern software design, testing, and deployment across a range of sectors.

Later Developments in the Field of Software Engineering:

Beyond her innovative work on the Apollo missions, Margaret Hamilton made significant contributions to software engineering in the following years.

In her capacity as the creator and CEO of Hamilton Technologies, Inc., she persisted in her support of strict software development procedures and spearheaded innovations in safety-critical systems and software reliability.

Hamilton's involvement in numerous government and commercial projects focused at enhancing software quality and cybersecurity can be attributed to her skill in software engineering.

Her pioneering work in the industry has left a lasting legacy that will influence software engineering for years to come by motivating new generations of engineers to place a high value on innovation, dependability, and robustness in their work.

CHAPTER 4: ARCHITECT OF THE INTERNET, RADIA PERLMAN

The Spanning Tree Protocol's creation:

When Radia Perlman developed the Spanning Tree Protocol (STP), she overcame a major obstacle in network architecture and completely changed computer networking.

As networks becoming more complicated in the early 1980s, broadcast storms caused by network loops posed a hazard to communication. This issue was deftly resolved by Perlman's STP algorithm, which found and disabled redundant paths in a network to guarantee a topology free of loops while preserving fault tolerance.

Ethernet networks' scalability and stability were made possible via STP, which has now become a pillar of contemporary network protocols.

Perlman's groundbreaking work shaped the modern architecture of the internet by laying the groundwork for later developments in network redundancy and resilience.

She has received multiple awards for her contributions to computer networking, solidifying her reputation as a trailblazer in the industry.

Contributions to the Design of Networks:

The impact of Radia Perlman's contributions on network architecture is extensive and profound.

In addition to creating the ground-breaking Spanning Tree Protocol (STP), Perlman has significantly advanced a number of other areas of network architecture.

Her contributions include the creation of the TRILL (Transparent Interconnection of Lots of Links) protocol, which enables multi-pathing and loop avoidance in massive data centers, hence improving the scalability and efficiency of Ethernet networks.

In addition to enhancing computer networks' dependability and efficiency, Perlman's contributions to network design have opened the door for the creation of cutting-edge inventions like Software-Defined Networking (SDN) and Network Function Virtualization (NFV).

Her reputation as a trailblazing personality in the field of network engineering has had a lasting impact on how contemporary networking has developed.

Thoughts on Women in Tech:

The significance of diversity and inclusivity in the computer industry is emphasized by Radia Perlman's observations on women in the area.

Perlman is a well-known female engineer in a field that has historically been dominated by men. She is an advocate for the development of welcoming workplaces where women can flourish and make significant contributions to technology.

She highlights that in order to inspire more women to seek professions in STEM, networking, mentorship, and dismantling gender stereotypes are essential. Inspired by her own experience, Perlman shows that a person's gender shouldn't ever be a hindrance to their success in the technology industry.

Perlman continues to promote equality and diversity through her advocacy and example, which is propelling positive change in the IT sector.

CHAPTER 5: ANITA BORG, A CHAMPION FOR WOMEN IN COMPUTING

Establishing the Center for Women and Technology:

An important turning point in the promotion of gender equality in the computer industry was the foundation of the Institute for Women and Technology (IWT) by Anita Borg.

In order to address concerns of representation, access, and progress, Borg founded the IWT in 1997 after realizing the systemic impediments that women in technology faced.

The institution, which provides research, advocacy, and community-building programs, acted as a catalyst for projects encouraging women's leadership and engagement in STEM professions.

Borg promoted cooperation between business executives, academics, and legislators through the IWT in order to advance structural change and establish more welcoming work conditions for women in technology.

The landscape of diversity and inclusion is being shaped by Borg's vision and dedication to elevating women in IT, providing a lasting legacy of advancement and opportunity for future generations of female technologist.

Establishment of the Grace Hopper Celebration:

The Grace Hopper Celebration (GHC), founded by Anita Borg, is a ground-breaking program that encourages diversity and inclusion in the computer sector.

GHC, named for the trailblazing computer scientist Grace Hopper, grew to be the largest assembly of women technologists globally, offering a forum for mentoring, education, and networking.

Borg saw GHC as a venue to address structural issues, promote gender parity, and honor the accomplishments of women in technology.

Borg made a lasting contribution to the fight for more opportunities and representation for women in the technology industry by creating a welcoming environment at GHC where they could interact, collaborate, and gain confidence from one another.

Ongoing Effect on Diversity in Technology:

Long after her death, Anita Borg's influence on diversity in technology will continue to grow.

Borg created the foundation for structural transformation in the tech sector with her tireless activism and innovative leadership.

Her legacy endures in the work that empowers women and underrepresented groups in technology through programs like the Grace Hopper Celebration and institutions like the Anita Borg Institute.

Borg's focus on networking, mentoring, and fostering inclusive environments has motivated a great number of people to question the status quo and seek jobs in STEM sectors. Borg's impact continues to alter the trajectory of diversity and inclusion in tech, paving the way for a more innovative and fair future by elevating different voices and advocating for equity and representation.

CHAPTER 6: THE ACTRESS WHO BECAME AN INVENTOR, HEDY LAMARR

The creation of the frequency-hopping spread spectrum:

The frequency-hopping spread spectrum (FHSS), invented by Hedy Lamarr, was a ground-breaking invention that transformed communication technology.

Renowned actress Hedy Lamarr and composer George Antheil worked together to create a covert communication system during World War II that prevented Nazi attempts to jam radio-controlled torpedoes.

They developed a technique for quickly switching frequencies to avoid interception, which laid the foundation for FHSS, after being inspired by player-piano rolls.

Despite the military's initial disregard for their creation, FHSS went on to play a crucial role in the development of contemporary wireless communication technologies like Wi-Fi, Bluetooth, and GPS.

Lamarr's groundbreaking work highlights the relationship between creativity and science and shows how interdisciplinary cooperation has a significant influence on technical innovation and the development of the digital era.

Appreciating the Contributions of Lamarr:

Hedy Lamarr's contributions to technology were only recently acknowledged, although her ground-breaking work eventually won her considerable praise.

She received the Electronic Frontier Foundation Pioneer Award in 1997 in recognition of her contribution to the creation of frequency-hopping spread spectrum (FHSS), the technology that served as the basis for contemporary wireless communication.

In 2014, Lamarr was posthumously admitted into the National Inventors Hall of Fame, a distinction that acknowledged her as a trailblazer in the realm of communication technology. Her life and accomplishments were also honored in a number of books and documentaries that highlighted her extraordinary mind and inventive spirit.

Lamarr's legacy as a Hollywood star and a technology forerunner has been appropriately entrenched via these honors, encouraging future generations to acknowledge the interplay between creativity and innovation in altering the world we live in today.

The impact on Contemporary Wireless Communications:

Hedy Lamarr has had a significant impact on contemporary wireless communication.

During World War II, she developed frequency-hopping spread spectrum (FHSS), which set the foundation for later technologies like Bluetooth, GPS, and Wi-Fi.

Lamarr and composer George Antheil devised a fast frequency switching technique that allowed them to establish a communication system impervious to interference and interception. This idea is now at the core of many modern wireless communication systems.

Lamarr's pioneering work and inventive attitude continue to influence the development of contemporary technology, emphasizing the lasting influence of interdisciplinary cooperation and the critical role that creativity plays in the advancement of communication technology.

CHAPTER 7: NASA'S TRAILBLAZING KATHERINE JOHNSON

Determining Space Mission Trajectories:

During her time working as a mathematician at NASA, Katherine Johnson was crucial in establishing the paths of space missions.

Renowned for her extraordinary aptitude in mathematics, Johnson designed the course for astronaut John Glenn's historic 1962 first-ever orbital space journey.

Her accurate calculations, which steered Glenn's spacecraft Friendship 7 around the Earth, were crucial to the mission's success and safety.

Beyond this significant accomplishment, Johnson continued to contribute by providing vital estimates for many more missions, such as the Apollo moon landing missions.

Johnson endured discrimination on the basis of race and gender, but her brilliance and commitment won her the respect and admiration of her peers, cementing her reputation as a pioneer in space exploration and encouraging upcoming generations to enter the STEM disciplines.

Apollo and Mercury Program Contributions:

Katherine Johnson's exceptional mathematics abilities allowed her to make significant contributions to the Mercury and Apollo programs.

As one of NASA's "human computers," Johnson was instrumental in determining the launch windows, orbital mechanics, and trajectories for the Mercury missions, which included astronaut Alan Shepard's historic flight—the first American in space.

Her calculations played a crucial role in guaranteeing these groundbreaking missions' safety and success.

Furthermore, Johnson supplied crucial calculations for the Apollo 11 mission's trajectory during the Apollo program, which resulted in the successful landing of the first humans on the Moon in 1969.

Johnson was acknowledged as a pioneer in the field of aerospace engineering and served as an inspiration to upcoming generations of scientists with her painstaking labor and unmatched accuracy, which were crucial to NASA's space exploration efforts.

Recognition in the Following Years:

Later on, Katherine Johnson was duly acknowledged for her innovative contributions to the field of space exploration.

President Barack Obama bestowed upon her the Presidential Medal of Freedom in 2015, the nation's highest civilian award.

This esteemed award brought attention to Johnson's outstanding accomplishments and her trailblazing position as an African American woman in the STEM areas.

Furthermore, Johnson's incredible tale was widely acknowledged by the 2016 movie "Hidden Figures," which introduced her accomplishments to a worldwide viewership. Johnson's reputation as a trailblazer and source of inspiration for upcoming generations is perpetuated by these accolades and acknowledgement.

CHAPTER 8: THE GAMING PIONEER, CAROL SHAW

Early Years of Video Game Development:

An important turning point in the history of the video game business was reached by Carol Shaw during the early years of her career.

Shaw joined Atari, Inc. in 1978, making her one of the first female video game designers.

One of the first instances of a three-dimensional video game, "3-D Tic-Tac-Toe," was made possible by her groundbreaking work.

Shaw stood out for her creative approach to game design and programming methods, which made her a trailblazer in an industry dominated by men.

Her contributions inspired diversity and creativity in a rapidly changing industry, laying the foundation for upcoming g enerations of game developers. Shaw's influence is still felt today, highlighting how crucial inclusion and representation are to influencing the video game production industry.

Generation of Innovative Titles:

A revolutionary period in the history of video games was heralded by Carol Shaw's creative generation of games.

Shaw had a significant effect as one of the first female video game designers. Her technical prowess and innovative spirit produced ground-breaking games that redefined the gaming industry.

"3-D Tic-Tac-Toe" established a new benchmark for immersive gaming by showcasing Shaw's early experiments with three-dimensional visuals.

Her most famous work, "River Raid," went on to become an immediate classic because to its action-packed storyline and creative level design.

Shaw transformed the gaming business and cleared the path for upcoming game creators with his ability to blend technological innovation with captivating gameplay mechanics. Her pioneering legacy still encourages variety and inventiveness in modern video game design.

Girl in Gaming: Obstacles and Triumphs:

Being among the earliest female gamers, Carol Shaw encountered several obstacles.

She had to deal with sexism and gender bias in a male-dominated field, where she was frequently undervalued and ignored.

Shaw overcame these challenges thanks to her incredible talent and tenacity.

Her contributions as an early producer of video games, such as "River Raid" and "3-D Tic-Tac-Toe," broke stereotypes and opened doors for more female gamers in the future.

Shaw's fortitude in the face of hardship is an inspiration, emphasizing the role that diversity and inclusivity have in influencing the development of the gaming industry.

CHAPTER 9: SEARCH AND TECHNOLOGY INNOVATOR, MARISSA MAYER

Early Google Career:

Marissa Mayer's early work at Google was crucial in determining the course of her career and establishing her standing as a visionary in the digital industry.

Mayer joined Google in 1999 as the company's 20th employee and advanced fast through the ranks to take on the role of Vice President of Search Products and User Experience.

Her input was crucial to the creation of many well-known Google products, such as the well-known homepage, Google Maps, and Google Earth.

Mayer's strategic insights and acute sense of design and user experience helped Google become a global tech giant and reach new heights.

Her time at Google solidified her reputation as one of Silicon Valley's most prominent individuals and set the groundwork for her future leadership positions.

Yahoo!'s leadership!:

Marissa Mayer's tenure as Yahoo!'s CEO was an important, yet uneventful, chapter in her career.

After being named CEO of Yahoo! in 2012, Mayer set out to turn around the struggling digital company. Yahoo! saw a number of acquisitions and product redesigns under her direction, including the redesigned Yahoo! Mail and Yahoo! News.

Mayer endeavored to establish Yahoo! as a participant in the dynamic digital terrain. But despite early hope, difficulties remained, and Yahoo!'s main business was still up against competition.

Mayer's time at Yahoo! ultimately came to an end in 2017 when Verizon acquired the company. Even though Mayer's leadership at Yahoo! came under fire, her innovations in technology and her status as the first female CEO are still important in the history of the business.

Views Regarding Women in Leadership:

Marissa Mayer's viewpoint on women in leadership emphasizes how crucial it is to dismantle obstacles and promote diversity.

Mayer, one of the few female CEO's in the tech sector, is an advocate for the advancement of women and their representation in positions of leadership.

She is an advocate for dispelling myths and fostering welcoming settings that support the success of women.

Mayer's personal experience as a tech executive serves as an example, highlighting the importance of varied viewpoints and the ongoing need to advance gender equality in the workplace.

Mayer continues to open doors for upcoming generations of women leaders in technology and other fields with her advocacy and leadership.

CHAPTER 10: CRYPTOGRAPHY'S PIONEER, SHAFI GOLDWASSER

A Contribution to the Theory of Complexity:

Shafi Goldwasser has made significant and wide-ranging contributions to the field of complexity theory.

Goldwasser is a well-known mathematician and computer scientist who has made substantial strides in our knowledge of computational issue complexity.

Her seminal work has revolutionized the fields of complexity theory, cryptography, and interactive proofs, especially in the area of probabilistically checkable proofs (PCP's) and interactive proofs.

Goldwasser's work has cleared the path for the creation of new cryptographic protocols and algorithms while also helping to clarify important issues about the intrinsic difficulty of computational jobs.

Her groundbreaking discoveries continue to influence complexity theory research and development, influencing computation and information security in the future.

Employment in Security and Cryptography:

Modern information security procedures have been shaped by Shafi Goldwasser's groundbreaking work in cryptography and security.

Goldwasser, being a trailblazing scientist in the domain, has achieved noteworthy advancements in the creation of cryptographic methods that guarantee the privacy, accuracy, and legitimacy of digital information.

Her research has laid the theoretical groundwork for secure communication and computation in the digital age in fields including probabilistically checkable proofs, zero-knowledge proofs, and secure multi-party computation.

In addition to advancing the subject of cryptography, Goldwasser's work has had practical applications, influencing the creation of cryptographic algorithms and protocols that serve as the foundation for widely used secure communication systems.

Her observations continue to spur innovation in cybersecurity by tackling new risks and guaranteeing the security of private data in a society growing more interconnected by the day.

Acknowledgment and Trophy:

Shafi Goldwasser has received many important accolades and medals for her groundbreaking work in computer science and cryptography.

For her groundbreaking work in complexity theory and cryptography, she was given the Turing Award in 2012—the highest honor in computer science.

In addition, Goldwasser has won the IEEE Emanuel R. Piore Award, the RSA Award in Mathematics, the ACM Grace Murray Hopper Award, and the Gödel Prize.

Her standing as a leading figure in her industry is further cemented by her membership in the National Academy of Sciences, the American Academy of Arts and Sciences, and the National Academy of Engineering.

CHAPTER 11: ARTIFICIAL INTELLIGENCE LEADERSHIP BY FEI-FEI LI

Studies on AI and Computer Vision:

Fei-Fei Li's work in artificial intelligence (AI) and computer vision has revolutionized the field, improving machines' ability to recognize and comprehend visual data.

Li is a leading authority in the field, and the focus of her work is on creating models and algorithms that let computers comprehend situations, identify objects, and interpret photos as accurately as humans can.

Among her groundbreaking accomplishments is the creation of massive datasets like ImageNet, which are essential for computer vision system training and benchmarking.

Li's work has significant ramifications in a number of fields, including robotics, augmented reality, driverless cars, and healthcare. Li's inventive work pushes the limits of AI and computer vision, advancing the development of machines that are more powerful and intelligent.

Google and Stanford Leadership:

Fei-Fei Li's innovative approach to AI research and education has distinguished her leadership at Google and Stanford Universities.

Li led innovative research projects as the director of the Stanford Artificial Intelligence Lab (SAIL) and the Stanford Vision Lab, encouraging faculty and student cooperation and creativity.

Her impact was further cemented during her stint at Google as Chief Scientist of AI/ML, where she oversaw projects to incorporate AI into a range of Google services and products.

Li's leadership has been distinguished by a dedication to bridging the gap between academics and industry, promoting diversity and inclusion in the field, and developing AI technology in a responsible and ethical manner. Li continues to influence AI research and education through her leadership, motivating the following generation of AI innovators.

Promoting Ethical AI:

Fei-Fei Li is a well-known proponent of moral AI methods. Li highlights the significance of creating artificial intelligence (AI) technologies that put an emphasis on accountability, transparency, and fairness through her research and leadership positions at Google and Stanford University.

In order to address the societal repercussions and biases in AI systems, she is an advocate of interdisciplinary collaboration and ethical principles.

In order to further AI research while guaranteeing its ethical and societal impact, Li co-founded the Stanford Institute for Human-Centered Artificial Intelligence (HAI).

Li is influencing the global community to give ethics a priority in the development of artificial intelligence through her initiatives and reshaping the discourse around responsible AI development.

CHAPTER 12: RESHMA SAUJANI, ENCOURAGING WOMEN IN TECH

Founders of Girls Who Code:

The establishment of Girls Who Code by Reshma Saujani has significantly contributed to the reduction of the gender gap in technology.

Seeing how few women work in computer science, Saujani founded Girls Who Code in 2012 with the goal of encouraging young girls to seek professions in technology.

Females who code gives females access to computer science education and chances for skill development through creative programs and initiatives.

Girls Who Code has reached thousands of girls globally and is changing the face of technology by promoting diversity and inclusion thanks to Saujani's vision and leadership.

Her activism keeps dismantling obstacles and paving the way for girls to prosper in the digital era.

Promoting Equity in STEM Education:

Reshma Saujani is a devoted champion of fairness in STEM education, especially for women and marginalized groups.

Saujani has spearheaded efforts to reduce the gender gap in technology by giving access to computer science education and chances for skill development through her nonprofit, Girls Who Code.

Girls Who Code provides girls with resources, coaching, and free coding training to enable them to pursue jobs in STEM subjects.

Through her efforts, Saujani has changed the face of STEM education, increased the number of young women entering the tech sector, and made sure that everyone has an equal chance to prosper in the digital era.

Her efforts continue to motivate and spur change, advancing the creation of a more just and inclusive society.

Effect on Narrowing the Gender Gap in Tech:

The significant efforts of Reshma Saujani, especially through Girls Who Code, have been crucial in reducing the gender disparity in the technology industry.

Through the provision of computer science education, mentorship, and skill development opportunities, Saujani has enabled numerous young women to aspire to jobs in STEM disciplines.

Her advocacy has caused a cultural shift, dispelling myths and removing obstacles that have historically prevented girls from pursuing careers in technology.

In addition to increasing the number of women in technology, Saujani's initiatives have diversified viewpoints and promoted creativity.

Saujani keeps advancing the cause of a more egalitarian and inclusive tech sector through her activities.

CONCLUSION: CONTINUING THE TRADITION

One thing becomes clear when we consider the inspirational journeys of trailblazers like Ada Lovelace, Grace Hopper, and Carol Shaw, as well as the visionary leadership of modern figures like Fei-Fei Li, Shafi Goldwasser, and Reshma Saujani: their legacies are not just tales of individual achievement, but also rays of hope that point us in the direction of a future where diversity is valued as our greatest asset and innovation knows no bounds.

As we carry on their legacy, let us embrace the values of inclusivity, curiosity, and tenacity, understanding that every success and every obstacle overcome opens the door to a better tomorrow.

In order to commemorate their legacy, let's dare to dream big, to upset the status quo, and to build a society in which everyone has the opportunity to shape the course of history.

ACKNOWLEDGMENTS

I want to express my sincere gratitude to everyone who has helped me along the way: friends and family who have never wavered in their support, mentors who have offered advice, and coworkers who have offered support.

Your confidence in me has been my driving force, encouraging me to overcome every challenge and soar to new heights.

We have set out on a journey of learning, creativity, and exploration together, and for that, I am incredibly appreciative of your unshakable faith and commitment.

This work is the result of our combined efforts, and I am grateful that I was able to embark on this journey with each and every one of you.

ABOUT THE AUTHOR

As the writer, my motivation comes from a love of language and an insatiable curiosity about a wide range of subjects.

Having studied creative writing, technology, and literature in the past, I enjoy telling stories that enthrall and motivate people.

My passion to tell stories that genuinely connect with readers has driven me to explore language, culture, and ideas in a dynamic way throughout my writing career.

I want to cross boundaries with the feelings, ideas, and dialogues I aspire to with my work.

I want to make a lasting impression and deeply connect with readers with every article I write, leaving them feeling enlightened and nourished.

www.ingramcontent.com/pod-product-compliance
Lightning Source LLC
Chambersburg PA
CBHW062123220526
45471CB00010B/3855